If it happened here
    as it happened there...
If it happened now
    as it happened then...

Who would have seen the miracle?
Who would have brought gifts?
Who would have taken Them in?

First printing.

Published in Canada by
Tundra Books of Montreal
Montreal, Quebec H3G 1J6
ISBN 0-88776-071-6

Legal deposit, Third Quarter
Quebec National Library

Published in the United States by
Tundra Books of Northern New York
Plattsburgh, New York 12901
ISBN 0-912766-41-7
Library of Congress Card No. 76-23274

Transparencies by T.E. Moore, Toronto. Typeset in 12 on 16 Palatino by Compoplus, Montreal, Canada. Printed by Pierre Des Marais, Inc., Montreal, Canada. Bound by A. Horowitz & Son. William Kurelek is represented by the Isaacs Gallery, Toronto.

PRINTED IN CANADA

A Northern Nativity

Christmas dreams of a prairie boy

William Kurelek

Tundra Books

Times were hard that Christmas during the Depression of the 1930's when William was twelve years old.

Everywhere across the country men traveled in search of work. They begged food, slept wherever they found shelter, rode boxcars — led on always by the hope that in the next town they would find a job and money to send to wives and children back home. Some families had lost their homes and they traveled in broken-down cars, trusting to the kindness of strangers to keep going...

Outside the prairie was covered with snow. Toward eleven o'clock William ventured out of the warm farmhouse kitchen up the dark stairway to his cold bedroom. Swiftly he stripped down to his long johns, dived between the icy sheets and pulled the covers over his head. Curled into a ball like a hibernating animal, he breathed and breathed until he felt warm enough under the blankets to relax and stretch out.

William enjoyed watching himself fall asleep, going back over the events of the day and seeing them slowly take on a new life in his dreams. In school that day his class had begun rehearsing for the annual Christmas concert. "And Heaven and Nature sing... and Heaven and Nature sing"... the words of the carol still rang in his head. And at Sunday school that week the teacher had retold the Christmas story — of a Child born into a Jewish family almost 2000 years ago, faraway across the sea in a little town called Bethlehem. He was a very special child. That was why, even though He was born in a stable, all kinds of people came to see Him, the skies opened and choirs of angels sang "Glory to God in the highest and on earth peace to men of good will."

As drowsiness came over William, the Nativity story got mixed up with his history and geography lessons, and he had his first Christmas dream. It was about the Far North, perhaps because his nose protruded from the bedcovers and breathed the cold crisp air in the bedroom.

Throughout that December when he was twelve years old he had these Christmas dreams. A few were long; others were more like pictures that flashed on very briefly. But they all started and ended with the questions:

If it happened there, why not here?
If it happened then, why not now?

1. The Holy Family as Eskimo

Against a deep black sky, the northern lights play — and the perpetual night of outer space is pricked with the sharp jabs of a million stars. Fluted snow fields stretch toward the horizon where hummocky crags of ice have been piled up by the crunch of the tide against the land. In a seal hunter's half-igloo shelter sit a woman and child. The child is fondling a roly-poly husky pup. Nearby, a fur-clad man is tending some sleigh dogs. Around his head, a strange light flickers. It also surrounds the faces of the mother and child.

A surge of excitement fills William as he recognizes the Holy Family — the simple, saintly Joseph; the Virgin Mary, gentlest of mothers; and the Infant Jesus, the Son of God Himself.

William feels an urge to sing in celebration of the scene. But the words of the carol come out jumbled… "And Arctic nature sings, and Arctic nature sings…" He sees himself asleep at the edge of the dream, and he wants to wake himself up so that he will remember forever the picture and the joy it brought him.

2.   The Cowboys' Christmas

A big herd of short-horned beef cattle mills around near the winter feeding enclosure. Gray skies drop the first feathery flakes of a second snowfall. Silhouetted against the distant foothills of the Rocky Mountains are three cowhands on horseback. A fourth is urging his horse through the herd, trying to move the cows in the right direction.

William loved to read about cowboys, and now in his dream he finds himself watching them as they go about their work. Suddenly, his attention is diverted to his left. A Presence seems to shine through the boards of the feeding stall. He kneels to peek through a knothole. There They are, the Mother and Child, alone among the hay bales. And strange waves of light circle Their heads.

His heart skips in anticipation. Would his cowboy heroes visit the Child as the shepherds had in Bethlehem, and would the cowboys invite Them into the warmth of the bunkhouse? These men know what it is like to be out in the cold. He sees them huddled in their sheepskin coats, more anxious than usual to complete the roundup. They are looking forward to the cheer of a big Christmas party with plenty of food and drink.

He picks up courage and tries calling to the men on horseback to come and see what he sees. They pay no attention to him whatever. Are they too tough, too hard to share his vision? Or is his voice too weak to be heard above the bawling of the herd?

3.   The Rod Rider's Christmas

William saw himself in this dream as Bill, the young man he wanted to be when he was old enough to do as he pleased. But this Bill is bent over and dejected like an old man. It is the wrong time to be young, ambitious and full of hope. Beyond the railway tracks in this big city at the edge of the Prairies stand sheds and silos, many of them dark and closed. Bill is one of the unemployed swarming out of boxcars, begging lodging and food, looking cold and discouraged. "Someday," his teacher had said while explaining the Depression to William's class, "you may taste despair — and then you will know how much kindness can mean."

Bill knocks at several houses along the tracks to try to get shelter. At the last door the lady who turns him away mutters, "Lazy bums!" He crosses the tracks to try on the other side, boiling with anger: "I am *not* lazy. Ukrainians have always worked hard." And then he remembers! Tonight is January 6, the Ukrainian Christmas Eve. This is Bill's first Christmas away from home, family and the Holy Feast of twelve dishes. He feels as low as he ever imagined possible.

Just then he hears singing, and it is in Ukrainian! *Boh Predvichney* — God Eternal — was a carol sung by children going from house to house in the old country. But these are strong men's voices, coming from another line of boxcars. He loses no time scrambling over and introducing himself. It is a section foreman and his gang in a work car. "*Proshoo, Vitayemo,* spend the night in one of our bunks." The offer is made and gladly accepted.

As Bill settles in he wonders if he should tell them something he has just seen. At the very moment he heard them singing he was passing an open boxcar. A lantern had suddenly lit up the inside and he saw Mary wrapping the Child in a blanket on some packing straw while Joseph looked on protectively. Bill hadn't stopped though. Somehow he felt the vision was a sign to go on to the kindness he was to receive from these working men. And it was more: it was a happiness to treasure in his heart during these hard times.

Yet perhaps the working men would have believed — for they had shared with him the traditional Christmas fare from their lunch boxes.

4.   The Holy Family as Indian

In school that day, they'd learned a carol written by an early missionary for the Huron Indians in their own language. William knew it only in English:

It was in the moon of wintertime when all the birds had fled,
That mighty Gitchie Manitou sent angel choirs instead.
Before their light the stars grew dim
And wondering hunters heard the hymn —
Jesous, your king is born — Jesous Ahatonhia.

It was running through his head that night as a picture began to appear of an Indian trapper's hut in a northern spruce forest. Outside a man is stretching and scraping a skin. A little girl on snowshoes stares curiously at the Holy Family as They approach the door of her home to ask for shelter.

William doubts these people will accept the Child. Many cruel things have been done to native peoples by men who had His name on their lips but not in their hearts. Will that be forgiven now?

Then William realizes there is nothing to forgive — for the Holy Family standing at the door are Indians just as the family inside.

Jesous Ahatonhia
Jesous Ahatonhia
Jesous Ahatonhia

The Child's name fits beautifully into any language, for He comes as a light to all nations.

5. A Truckdriver's Charity

This dream was set in a mining town: William knew that from the piles of dark slag and the gray mining shaft sheds. Did several pictures of mining towns come together, William wondered, for mining and smelting aren't always done together.

Along the road in front of the chain-link fence the snow is dirty from the smelter's chimneys. In the foreground a battered old car has broken down and a man is under the hood trying to fix it. There is that special light playing about him, and about the Mother and Child in the car.

A truck rolls by. William does not expect it to stop and is surprised when it pulls up a few yards down the road. The driver gets out and, carrying his tool kit, walks back toward Joseph.

Did he realize who he was helping, William wondered, on waking. Perhaps it didn't matter — would not the Child one day proclaim: "Believe Me when you did it to one of the least of My brethren, you did it to Me." If the driver helped everyone in trouble, wasn't he helping the Holy One?

6.   In the Mountains

This dream found William in high mountain country, breathtaking and awesome in its majesty.

Below him evergreens rise tall out of the sunlit snow. And far beyond, the peaks of another much more massive range shine against a cloudless blue sky. To his surprise words come to William to explain the beauty he sees: ''Only a Creator who is beauty itself can create beauty — only those who are made in His image can appreciate that beauty.''

William finds himself searching the landscape, not for rocks, trees, eagles or mountain goats, but for people with whom to share his appreciation. Dreams have a way of fulfilling the dreamer's fears or wishes. Soon he begins to see skiers enjoying their Christmas vacation on the snowy slopes. But just as he decides to approach them he notices Mary and the Child. They are riding a packhorse led by Joseph over the difficult trail. They are obviously heading for the ski chalet which nestles luxuriously in the valley to the right. Will They be welcomed if They do not come as skiers?

William woke up wondering what the chalet operator was going to say to the Family. And would he himself have recognized Them if he had been one of the skiers?

7.   Two Barns

Mary and the Child are resting in the mountains in the straw of an abandoned barn.

Through the open side of the barn, traffic can be seen speeding by on a new highway. Some cars pull in at a neighboring barn that has been turned into an antique shop. The shoppers are searching for beauty from the past to give their lives interest. Yet none thinks of looking up to the other old barn; none seems aware of the very source of beauty so close by.

William feels moved to intrude into the scene. He walks quietly, so as not to disturb the Mother kneeling in adoration before her Babe. On the old timbers where children and tourists have carved their initials, he uses his jackknife to carve the words of a saint of old:

    Late have I loved you
    O ancient Beauty ever old and ever new.

8. A Farm Family's Adoration

A glorious winter sunset is turning the snow's crust a blue-mauve. Inside the farmhouse a window perfectly frames the parish church, whose tall thin steeple dominates the houses of the village.

The Holy Family has stopped for shelter in this modest dwelling. Joseph is now out on a job, happy knowing that Mother and Child are safe. William watches the farm family kneel in adoration of the Child.

A crucifix is plainly in view on the farmhouse wall. It is a sign that the Child will one day make the world the greatest gift He can — His life. This family owns little, but they too give gladly. The Child holds the world in His hands pointing to the places in it needing special help. The family is saving penny by penny day by day to buy medicines, food, clothing for the poor abroad, for there is hardship everywhere. They are making their offerings to Him now.

As William woke he recalled that the Christmas tree had stood not before but behind the Holy Family. He remembered a poem he had heard:

> Lead us away from the Christmas tree,
> Lead us back to the Christmas cave.
> If we have gifts to give
> Teach us to give to the hungry, the poor, the sick, the lame.

9.   Across the River from the Capital

The sky is starless, and snow threatens again. In the dark river below a boom of logs floats. Across the river a light shines in the tower of the capital, announcing to the country that its representatives are inside deliberating.

As William fumbles his way through the trees in this dream he almost trips over the body of a young man in a green army sleeping bag. William often daydreamed of hoboing around the country when he was old enough; he now recognizes himself as the young man Bill, trying to save money by sleeping in the open.

Before he has a chance to study Bill closely, he sees a light approaching. He hides to watch what will happen. It is Mary carrying a kerosene lantern in one hand, her other arm free to cradle her Child. She stops when she sees the sleeping figure and kneels beside it, putting down her lamp. She lets the Child stretch forth His little hand and gently touch the forehead of the sleeper. Bill frowns and mumbles, "Buzz off, will you!" He is proud of his young manhood, of going where he pleases, of owing no one anything.

"That can't be me. I'll never reject Him!" William cried out so loudly he woke himself up. In his dreams he wanted everyone to recognize and accept the Child. But was he really ready to give up his dream of independence? He stared at the ceiling a long time wondering about himself and about the people on the hill. What if the Child reached out to touch them?

10.   A Boathouse Man's Excuse

The Holy Family is fleeing by water. Joseph has moored his small covered fishing
boat to the wharf of a boathouse. He is wearing the black oilskins of a fisherman and
William wouldn't have recognized him were it not for the aura about him. Joseph
climbs the ladder and knocks at the door of the boathouse.

The boathouse man opens the door and Joseph comes right out with his troubles. He
needs fuel but he has no money. He has a job lined up where he is heading and on
his return he will repay all help received. The man just stares at Joseph. Then his face
darkens into a frown. But he doesn't come right out with "no"; instead he scolds
Joseph, "You didn't tie your boat properly — it's drifting off!" He sees neither the
length of the tethering rope nor the miraculous calm that surrounds the boat where
Mary is tending her Babe in complete security. Suddenly he seems to think of a way
to get rid of Joseph. "Try that house over there. They're better able to help." William
sees it across the water. A strong wind is snapping garments on a long clothesline
that suggests a large family.

William sensed the boathouse man was right without realizing it. William
remembered a saying of his father: "If you want something done, ask a busy man.
The others haven't got time."

11.   The Crib in the Garage

This dream put William in a small country town across from a filling station and garage. Grain elevators looming against the faint light of early dawn tell him he is in the West. There has been a light snowfall, and now it is very cold. The Holy Family stop at the only motel in town hoping to spend the night there. "Sorry," says the man at the desk pointing to the No Vacancy sign. "Business is usually slow in winter, but it's Christmas travel time, you know."

Joseph next stops his truck for gas, just before closing time, and asks the service station attendant if he knows where They can stay. "You're welcome to put up right here if you like. It's not much, I know, but at least you'll be warm." The town is still asleep. Only William stands outside, mindless of the cold, watching the Holy Family through the paneled panes of the garage door. The Child is sleeping peacefully in a car cot, and Mary and Joseph are chatting quietly and contentedly.

"So it is true, what they say about Western hospitality," William rejoiced, remembering the scene, and then as an afterthought: "Strange, I'd never thought of a garage as being a beautiful building."

12. The Gifts of the Fishermen

This was one of William's happiest Christmas dreams even though the setting was a bleak one.

It is the Atlantic coast, rocky and barren. The mist has just lifted. Clinging to the cliffs is an old hut used by fishermen to store fish that have dried on the rocks.

Boatloads of fishermen in black rubber nor'westers are arriving. Each boat docks at the foot of a flimsy-looking ladder which the men use to scale the rock. All of them carry small offerings of fish — the one gift they are able to bring to Mary and her Child. As they kneel in adoration, Mary holds up the Child for them to see.

How had they heard of the Child's presence on their shores, William wondered. Had the angels announced it to them as to the shepherds? Or was it something from the heart? Or a belief in miracles? A deep-sea fisherman faces death each time he goes out to sea — perhaps this is why he is more in tune than others with the Source of life.

William thought about it a long time after he woke.

13. Grain Elevator's Blind Corner

William knew the setting for this dream well. It was a grain elevator like the one he had hauled grain to with his father. There was the wagon still tilted after emptying its load into the elevator that would carry the grain to the top of the silo.

Through the open door of another grain elevator he sees Mary and the Child huddling in an alcove of the cold, unheated building. Why don't They go into the warmth of the engine room or office, he wonders.

Now that the grain wagon is empty the children beyond the door will be hitching their sleighs to it for free rides. They seem to be calling the Child to come out and play. Now that's silly. Can't they see that He is too young? How can they be so stupid?

Thinking about it later, William wondered if the whole dream was a tease. Then slowly its meaning came through to him. Wasn't it similar to another question often asked: "Why can't the sick in mind pull themselves together?"

14.   At the Falls

Dreams are muddled things. Times get all mixed up. Far separated places blend into one. Two or more different people seem to be one and the same. The impossible becomes possible and — strangely — the possible often becomes impossible.

In this dream, William sees the greatest falls in North America. It has been colder than usual that winter, and the falls have frozen. Here and there he sees cascading water with mist rising from it. The rest is an enormous jumble of icebergs and convoluted snowbanks stretching across the gorge, dazzling in the winter sun. Hundreds of people have come to see the magnificent sight: they lean against the railing, taking pictures and commenting to each other on the beauty before them.

Then William sees two figures in the background. It is Mary holding up the Infant so He too can see the ice marvel. For a moment They seem like any mother and child in the crowd. But They aren't just any mother and child. And William knows it. He tries to get the attention of the crowd. "Turn and look. You're missing the Creator for the creation..." but William can't wake the people. He only woke himself from his dream.

15.   The Holy Family as Black

Outside the snow is blowing and piling up on the window ledges. The room is large and drab: someone has tried to brighten it with decorations and banners. At long tables, poorly dressed men of all ages dig into a generous serving of Christmas turkey with the trimmings. Waiting on them, dressed in blue uniforms, are men who have chosen to give up their Christmas — a day off for most people — in the service of others. The Holy Family is sitting at the table too. The lines "inasmuch as you did it to the least of these…" would seem to explain this scene.

But there is something more to William's dream, something deeper which the men in blue have grasped. Looking closely, he notices that the Family's skin is black.

16.   The Presentation to the Children

William was thinking before he fell asleep:

On the first Christmas the Child was seen and recognized only by certain people. It couldn't have had anything to do with how rich they were or how powerful or how well educated. For what after all did the shepherds and the three kings have in common?

The first thing William saw when he fell asleep was a church on a low hill. It is milder here than in most of the northern land; snow is melting in patches to show the island's red soil. A mother and some children are kneeling before an outdoor crèche to admire it and say a prayer.

Suddenly the church door opens and Mary comes out smiling with the Child. The Child stretches His arms out to greet and bless the family. Their faces light up in easy recognition as if they knew that He was inside there all the time.

How was that possible, William wondered. "Except ye become as little children..." the words of Scripture came to him when he awoke.

17.   The Nightwatchman's Christmas

It was still pitch dark outside as William slept. But in his dream day is breaking over a prairie city. At a construction site, dark shapes of cranes and lifts are etched against the sky. Work has not started yet, but William makes out two men already on the job site. They are warming their hands over a makeshift brazier — a fuel barrel punched full of holes and fired with off cuts from concrete forms. One of them must be the nightwatchman. The other, the one with the beard, looks new to the country — a recent immigrant possibly. William draws nearer to the pair and recognizes the bearded man as Joseph.

To the watchman Joseph might be just another job hunter. But he pretends he is glad of his company. As he chats with Joseph he manages to give him many valuable tips that will help him get a job when the boss arrives at the work site.

Until that moment William was looking round in vain for Mary and the Child. Then he notices the door to the construction site office is open. Women and children certainly wouldn't be allowed in there. Yet there They are, the Holy pair basking in the warmth of the trailer's heater. Mary is wearing the embroidered blouse of a Slavic peasant woman.

Dimly William grasped the enigma of the situation: The watchman was conscientious. He shouldn't have let Them in, and yet he did.

18. Manger in a Lumber Camp Stable

It is a bright, sunny Christmas afternoon. Icicles are dripping from a lumber camp stable roof. In the distance lumberjacks are streaming out of their bunkhouses heading for the work shack. The cookie has just begun calling them to lunch on the camp gong. On an ordinary day most lumberjacks would be eating lunch right on their work strips from their lunch boxes. But obviously they have taken the day off to celebrate Christmas.

The stableman has gone off to join the celebration at the cook-house, leaving the doors at both ends open to air the stable. Through the rear doorway William can see Mary wrapping the Child in swaddling clothes and laying Him in a horse manger.

William learned at Sunday school that it was quite in keeping with the humility of the Christ Child that He should enter the world in such humble surroundings. William felt good about them being in there. He'd always liked the barn smells on his father's farm — the odor of straw, hay, chop, manure. The breath of the animals and the heat of their bodies keep a barn warm and cozy.

There was an old legend that farm animals could use human language at Christmas midnight: a reward given them on the first Christmas for accepting the Christ Child into their dwelling when people didn't. One Christmas midnight when William was younger he had sneaked into his father's barn. He didn't hear the animals speak, but he still liked the story.

19.   The Welcome at the Country Mission

It is evening. The sun is setting red, touching the snows of the countryside a delicate pink. A dilapidated blue car drives up to an old building which looks like something between a school and a farmhouse. A dog's barking announces the arrival to the people inside. They hurry out to embrace the newcomers warmly.

The place is a country mission, where the people have taken a Christian vow of poverty. They run their farm well but they are careful to keep it small so they do not make the mistake of worshiping gain. What they do not need they give to the poor families around them, or sell and use the money for their missionary work.

Why are these people not caught unawares by their Holy visitors? It is actually very simple. Inside the house near the doorway William finds a little notice which reads:

Receive every visitor as Christ Himself.

20.   Flight into a Far Country

William knew this would be his last dream.

On the first Christmas Joseph dreamed of an angel who told him to flee to a far country. Now the Holy Family is preparing to flee William's country too. They have been given a horse and buggy by a community of devout farming families.

They are off now and seem to be taking the warmth with Them as They disappear into the blowing snow. William had grown fond of Them as he followed Their fortunes throughout his country. Now he tries to run after Them, to beg Them to stay. But his legs sink deeper into the snow and he cannot move. He calls to Them in panic: "Please don't go!" This time he is heard. Their compassionate words float back to him through the blizzard: "We will return one day — when *you* are ready to receive Us with undivided love."

William woke shivering. His running in the dream had kicked the bedcovers to the floor. But the warmth of Their parting promise left him with enough peace to go back to restful sleep.

In his dreams William had always felt sorry when the Holy Family appeared and were not recognized or helped. Yet he was no readier than the people in his dreams to receive Them if it meant giving up his dream of independence.

Twenty years would pass, and he would grow to be a man, travel far, see many things and suffer much before he was ready for that promised day.

The Nativity dreams the boy William had when he was twelve years old were, of course, all based on pictures in his geography and history books, on stories he had heard, on Sunday school lessons and Bible readings in school.

As he grew older and became the young man Bill, he experienced many of the things he had dreamed of: traveling, hitching rides in boxcars, sleeping out because he had no money, working in a lumber camp, visiting the North. His paintings are therefore a combination of the places of his dreams and the places he saw.

The settings of the dreams

1. A classic igloo shelter used by Eskimo hunters in the Northwest Territories
2. Cattle country in Alberta and British Columbia
3. Winnipeg, Manitoba — freight yards of the 1930's
4. Indian trapper's encampment in Northern Quebec (Hymn of Father Brébeuf)
5. Near an iron mine, Flin Flon, Manitoba
6. Ski lodge in the Rockies, British Columbia
7. Near Lake Kamloops, British Columbia
8. Habitant family in old Quebec village
9. Across the river from Ottawa, Ontario
10. Peggy's Cove, Nova Scotia
11. Prairie town in Alberta
12. Fish-drying hut near Port-aux-Basques, Newfoundland
13. Grain elevator on the Prairies
14. Niagara Falls, Ontario
15. Salvation Army hostel in Halifax, Nova Scotia
16. Roman Catholic Church on Prince Edward Island
17. Construction site in Regina, Saskatchewan
18. Bush camp in New Brunswick
19. St. Benedict's Acres farm, operated by the Madonna House Apostate, Combermere, Ontario
20. Horse buggy of Old Order Mennonites, near Kitchener, Ontario

William Kurelek

William Kurelek grew up on the Prairies during the hard 1930's. He spent the first several years of his life on a grain farm in Alberta, Canada, where his father had settled after coming from the Ukraine. Then the family moved to a dairy farm in Manitoba, not far from the United States border. This is the setting of his award-winning books *A Prairie Boy's Winter* and *A Prairie Boy's Summer* and, in a way, of the present work: William's Christmas dreams took place in the cold upstairs bedroom of the farmhouse.

Later, to prove himself to his father and to finance his art studies, he worked in the lumber camps of northern Ontario and Quebec; this world, now passed into history, he re-created in another award-winning book, *Lumberjack*.

As a young man he traveled through Mexico and Europe before suffering an emotional breakdown in England, where he was hospitalized. He found in religion the strength to recover and to go on creating.

The Nativity has appeared in many Kurelek paintings. One large canvas shows the Madonna and Child being sheltered by a large haystack on a snow-covered prairie farm. Other paintings set the Nativity in his father's barn and in a railway shed. The collection of twenty paintings done by Kurelek for *A Northern Nativity* enlarges on his belief in the universality of the Christmas message.

William Kurelek is now Canada's best-known artist. His paintings are loved by thousands who have never set foot in an art gallery, and admired by art connoisseurs who have chosen them for major museums in Canada, the United States and Europe.